PROBLEM SOLVING CONNECTIONS

Dr. William Driscoll
Donald W. Robb

Orange Level

Charlesbridge

CONTENTS

Publisher: **Charlesbridge Publishing**
              85 Main Street, Watertown, MA 02472

Printed in the United States of America.

ISBN: 0-88106-650-8

10 9

UNIT 1

What Is Problem Solving?

You have been learning how to solve problems ever since you began your study of mathematics. In this unit, you will learn how to solve a special kind of problem called a *process problem*.

You will also learn how to find information by reading a problem carefully, and how to decide what you need to do in order to find the solution.

Learning more about the types of problems there are will help you to become an expert problem solver.

Is It a Problem?

Some of these examples are *problems* because they give us information and ask us to find an answer. Some of these examples are <u>not</u> *problems.*

Put a circle around the number of each example that <u>is</u> a *problem.*

1. 7
   + 3
   ___

2. $6 - 3 = 3$

3. $8 + 7 = ?$

4. 12
   + 8
   ___

5. $14 - 5 = ?$

6. $5 + 8 + 2 = ?$

7. 15
    18
     7
   + 4
   ___

8. Max had 4 apples. Lisa gave him 3 more. How many did he have then?

9. Kayla has 3 yellow crayons and 2 blue crayons.

10. Marco wants to buy a tape for $9.00. He has $6.00. How much more does he need to buy the tape?

11. Fred walks 6 blocks to school. Pilar walks 5 blocks.

12. Li-Ming collects baseball cards. Last week, her uncle gave her 5 new cards.

13. 2, 4, 6, ____ , ____ , ____

14. 6, 9, 12, ____ , ____ , ____

15. 25, 20, 15, ____ , ____ , ____

NAME________________________

What's Your Problem?

1. Make up a word problem for each number problem.

    Example A: $3 + 7 = ?$ Word Problem
    Mike had 3 tomatoes on one plant in his garden and 7 tomatoes on another. How many tomatoes did he have in all?

    Example B: $8 - 5 = ?$ Word Problem
    Sharon has 8 books. Randy has 5 books. Who has more books? How many more?

    a. $5 + 8 = ?$

    b. $7 - 3 = ?$

    c. $\$9.00 - \$4.00 = ?$

    d. $12 - 3 = ?$

    e. $5 + 3 + 2 = ?$

2. Now write four number problems of your own. Then write a word problem
   for each one.

Information, Please

1. Kevin collects model cars. He has 28 cars. Last week on his birthday his father gave him 2 more cars and his friend Ramon gave him another. Now how many does he have?

2. Misha wanted sweatshirt that cost $29.00. She has saved $18.00. How much more money will she need?

3. Last week during the magazine drive, Mark sold 7 subscriptions and Jenna sold 5. This week Mark sold 6 more and Jenna sold 9. In the two weeks, who sold more subscriptions?

4. Mr. Fisher brought in 14 new books for the classroom library. Janis took out 3 books. Paul, Yoshi, and Camille each took out 1 book. Eric took out 2 books. How many books were left?

5. Last week Molly scored 11 points in a basketball game. Yesterday she scored 8 points in the game and Sheila scored 6. How many more points did Molly score than Sheila in yesterday's game?

6. Jeremy, Rachel, and Verna were collecting cans of food to put in Thanksgiving baskets. Jeremy brought in 7 cans, Rachel brought in more cans than Jeremy, and Verna brought some in, too. How many cans did they have in all?

7. There are 27 students in Miss Hatfield's class. There are more girls than boys. How many boys are in the class?

8. Most days, 28 children ride Valerie's bus to school. The bus makes 8 stops between Valerie's corner and the school. On Robert's bus, there are 24 children. How many children ride the two buses?

9. Mr. Young is ordering chairs to replace the broken chairs in the third grade classrooms. The chairs in Mrs. Evan's room are 10 years old, and 4 of them are broken. Mr. Dunbar's chairs are 12 years old, and 6 of them are broken. If Mr. Young already has 3 new chairs, how many will he need to order?

10. Chuck wants to buy a birthday present for his cousin Marlene. He has $6.50 saved up. How much more will he need?

11. Mark's team played 7 games this season. They won last night's game by 3 runs. How many runs did Mark's team score in all?

NAME________________________

Choices, Choices, Choices

1. Charlie has blue socks and brown socks in his drawer. He doesn't separate the socks by pairs. It's dark in his bedroom when he gets dressed in the morning, so he takes his socks into the hall where there's more light to make sure he has a matching pair. What's the smallest number of socks that Charlie has to take out of the drawer to make sure he has a matching pair?

2. Akio and Yuki have a paper route that they work together. Akio delivers papers to 17 homes. Yuki delivers to 19 houses. How many customers do they have in all?

3. Mrs. Randolph asked Ann, Jan, and Nan to line up. How many different ways can the three girls line up?

4.   If Fran comes along and joins the line, how many ways are possible?

5.   In the equipment bag, Coach Markson has 2 orange balls, 4 green balls,
     and 3 red balls. How many balls will Coach Markson have to take out of
     the bag to make sure that she can give Carmen and Alicia each the same
     color ball?

Count the Possibilities

1. Melanie has four achievement awards – one each for Music, Writing, Soccer, and Art. Each one will take a full page in her scrap book. How many different ways can she put them in her book?

2. The third grade class is ordering T-shirts. The shirts are printed with a design that uses two colors, but you can choose from any combination of blue, red, and yellow. How many different two-color combinations could you order?

3. How many two-color combinations can you order if you can choose from blue, red, yellow, and green?

4. How many two-color combinations can you order if you can choose from
    blue, red, yellow, green, and orange?

5. How many two-color combinations can you order if you add purple to the
    list of choices?

Problem Solving

In our math class, we have been learning how to solve problems. We have solved math problems using addition and subtraction.

Now, we are beginning to work on solving "process problems." These are problems that cannot be solved just by adding or subtracting. They are the kind of problems that require critical thinking.

Students have to analyze the problems, select important information, organize the information, come up with a solution, and check to see if the solution really solves the problem.

Throughout the year, we'd like to share some of these problems with you so that you and your child can try them together at home.

Here are some problems like the ones we have just done in class. We think you'll enjoy solving them with your child.

One of the best ways for your child to understand these problems is to actually *do* them using real objects or making models. To help, we have included some suggestions for ideas to use with each problem.

1. Marge has a box of marking pens. In the box are some blue pens, some red pens, some yellow pens, and some green pens. How many pens will Marge have to take out of the box to be sure that she has at least two pens of the same color?

    SUGGESTION: *Use pens, pencils, or pieces of paper colored to represent the pens.*

2. At Stan's Pizza Shop, you can buy a small cheese pizza with two toppings
    for $4.79. If Stan has onions, peppers, sausage, and mushrooms as
    toppings, how many different combinations of two toppings could you
    buy?

    SUGGESTION: *Make a model, cut out paper for each topping, or try
    making a drawing.*

3. Ronnie saved his money to buy his brother a birthday present. The
    Bargain Store was having a sale, so Ronnie shopped there. He had
    $12.00 when he arrived at the store, and $1.00 left after he bought two
    presents. Which two items did he buy?

    SUGGESTION: *Use play money to help find the solution.*

SALE!

Soccer Ball	$5.00
Baseball Bat	$8.00
Model Airplane	$3.00
Jigsaw Puzzle	$2.00

UNIT 2

Using Strategies to Solve Problems

Now that you've learned about different kinds of problems, it's time to think about ways to solve problems.

Sometimes we cannot just add or subtract to solve a problem. Instead, we have to look for another way to find the solution. In this unit you will practice five different ways to think about problems. Each of these ways is called a *strategy*. A strategy means a way of thinking about something.

Strategies:

In this unit, you will learn about

1. Estimating
2. Acting Out
3. Making a Model
4. Solving a Simpler Problem
5. Working Backwards

NAME___________________________

At the Mall

1. Terry arrived at the mall with several coins in his pockets. He had quarters, dimes, and nickels. If he pulled three coins out of his pocket, how much money would he have in his hand?

   THINK: *What do you know? What do you need to know? Can you make a guess at the answer?*

2. The fruit store is having a sale. Colleen bought three different kinds of fruit for a fruit salad. In all, she bought five pounds for a party she was having. What is the least amount of money she could have spent?

green grapes	59¢/lb.
plums	79¢/lb.
bananas	49¢/lb.
apples	$ 1.19/lb.

3. The toy store had these items on sale:

Bag of balloons	59¢	Coloring book	$ 1.19
Wiffle Balls	$ 1.79	Crayons	89¢
Plastic truck	$ 3.49		

   Jorge has $3.00 to spend. What is the largest number of different things he can buy at the sale?

Bag of balloons	59¢	Coloring book	$ 1.19
Wiffle Balls	$ 1.79	Crayons	89¢
Plastic truck	$ 3.49		

4. Steve spent almost $6.50 for three items at the toy store sale. What items did he buy?

5. Candace bought two items at the toy store sale. One cost 90¢ more than the other. What items did she buy?

NAME______________________________

Join the Club

1. The Good Friends Club at Fairmont School begins each meeting with a handshake. Each member shakes hands with every other member. Last week, only Verna, Sulim, Pat, Karen, and Jonathan came to the meeting. How many handshakes were there?

   THINK: *Would it help if you and four friends all shook hands so someone could count the number of handshakes?*

2. At this week's meeting, 10 people showed up. How many handshakes were there this time?

3. Three of the club members – Larry, Michelle, and Trinh – volunteered to help at the School Fair. When they got to the fair, there were three jobs left to do – sell tickets, paint clown faces, and make popcorn. The three club members each chose the job they wanted to do. Larry chose first, then Trinh, and finally Michelle. How many choices did Larry have? How many did Trinh have? How about Michelle?

4. One arrangement the children may have chosen is that Michelle will sell tickets, Trinh will paint clown faces, and Larry will make popcorn. How many other ways could the children have chosen their jobs?

5. Latisha was standing in line to get tickets. Latisha was not first in line, but she wasn't last, either. There were three more people in front of her than behind her. What is the least number of people standing in line?

NAME________________________

Work It Out

1. Sally bought 10 gold links for a bracelet to give her mother. The links were on sale, but the jeweler charges for each cut he has to make to put the chain together. How many cuts will he charge her for?

    THINK: *Could you use strips of paper and make bracelet links to help you find the solution?*

2. To celebrate Sports Week, Mr. Kerr, the gym teacher, built a pyramid of basketballs outside the gym. He made four layers, with one basketball on the top layer. How many basketballs did he use in all?

3. Farmer Brown was on his way to market. With him was his dog Vern. Farmer Brown also had a bag of grain and a live chicken to sell. When he came to Big Muddy Creek, he found that the bridge was out and he had to wade across. His dog had never learned to swim, so he had to be carried across. Farmer Brown decided he could carry only one thing across at a time – either Vern, the chicken, or the bag of grain. He knew he would have to make several trips. Then he realized that he couldn't leave Vern and the chicken together on the same side of the river while he crossed with the grain because Vern was mean and hungry and would eat the chicken.

    Farmer Brown couldn't leave the chicken alone with the grain because the chicken would eat the grain, and Farmer Brown wouldn't be able to sell it at market.

    What could he do? How many times would he have to cross the stream?

4. Loida needed to measure some leaves for her science experiment. She couldn't find a ruler, but she did find some centimeter sticks. The sticks were not marked off in centimeter lengths, but some were 7-centimeter sticks and some 5-centimeter sticks.

She found a way to measure 10, 12, and 14 centimeters. She even found an easy way to measure 2 centimeters. How could she measure just 1 centimeter?

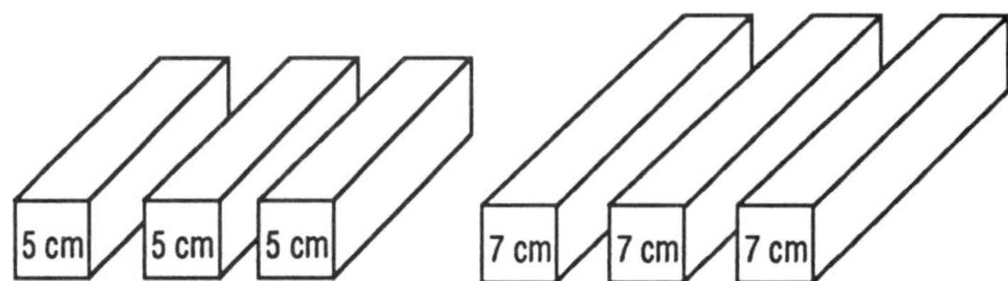

5. Here are several views of the same cube. Each face of the cube has a number on it. Can you tell what numbers belong on the two blank faces?

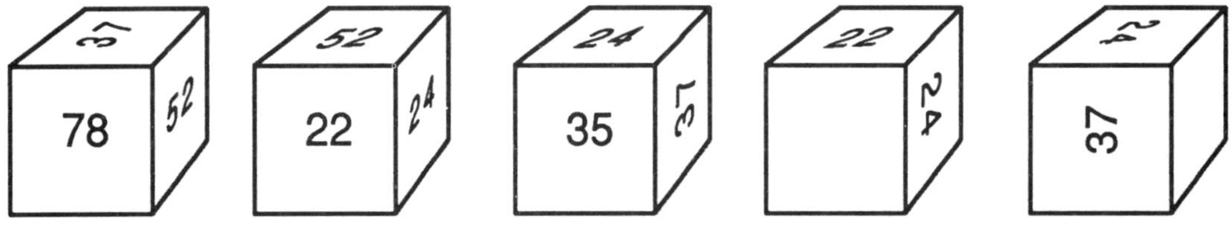

On Saturday

1. Saturday was Maggie's mother's birthday. Maggie's sister Karen and her brother Kevin had saved up some money for a present. Karen had $2.25 and Kevin had $3.65. The gift they wanted to buy cost $7.54, and Maggie said she would give them the rest of the money out of her piggy bank. She had just 11 coins in her bank. Did she have enough money to make up the difference?

    THINK: *What do you need to know before you can figure out if Maggie has enough?*

2. On Saturdays, Mrs. Fenton hires Freda to weed her four flower beds. Each bed takes half an hour to weed. She pays Freda $8.00 for the whole job. This Saturday, Freda had been working for an hour when her friend Seth came by. Seth helped her finish the job. How should they split the money Mrs. Fenton gave Freda?

3. Last Saturday, Owen's dad painted the front of the shed. He hired Owen to paint the other three walls. Each wall takes an hour to paint. Owen started at 2:00 and worked for an hour, finishing one side. Just then, his best friend Jimmy rode up on his bike. Jimmy agreed to help, so Owen and Jimmy did the back of the shed together. When they had finished, their friend Lori came along. All three of them worked on the last side of the shed. If they all worked steadily, did they finish the paint job before the rain started at 4:00?

4. Owen's dad had agreed to pay $18.00 for the paint job. Jimmy agreed to help because he needed $4.00 for a book he wanted. If Owen divided the money fairly, did Jimmy have enough for his book?

5. On Saturday afternoon, the Main Street bus picked up 16 passengers at its first stop. They all sat down, leaving 24 empty seats. At the second stop, 3 people got off and 8 got on. At the third stop, 2 people got off and 14 got on. At the next stop, no people got off and 12 got on. When the bus pulled away from this stop, how many passengers were standing, if all the seats were taken?

NAME_______________________

Challenge

1. The elevators in the Tower Building hold 15 people each. This afternoon, 9 people got onto one of the elevators at the ground floor. The elevator went to the 20th floor without stopping. There, 3 people got off and 5 got on. At the 21st floor, 8 got off and 6 got on. At the 22nd floor, 2 got off and 7 got on. At the 23rd floor, 4 people got off. There were 9 people waiting on that floor. Will they all be able to get on?

2. Greg's older brother Wayne bought a used car for $600.00, but sold it the same day for $700.00. Then he changed his mind, and that evening he bought it back again – for $800.00. Changing his mind again, he sold it the next morning for $900.00. On those deals, did Wayne make money, break even, or lose money? If he made or lost money, how much?

3. Warren wanted to buy colored stones for the bottom of his fish tank. At the pet supply store, stones were on sale.

Small gray stones 65 stones to the pound	$ 1.88/lb.
Medium pink stones 40 stones to the pound	$ 2.49/lb.
Large brown stones 15 stones to the pound	$ 2.98/lb.

If Warren spent $6.25, how many stones did he get, and what colors were they?

4. Wildwood Forest is a square 10 kilometers on a side. A road starts at the exact center of the forest. Instead of going straight north, south, east, or west to the edge of the forest, the road makes a lot of turns. It goes 1 kilometer north, then 2 kilometers west, 3 kilometers south, 4 kilometers east, 5 kilometers north, 6 kilometers west, 7 kilometers south, 8 kilometers east and north until it reaches the edge of the forest. On what side (north, south, east, or west) does the road reach the edge of the forest? How long is the road?

5. Ms. Collins, the gym teacher, and Mr. Lenox, the music teacher, are teaching the third graders a square dance. They selected four boys and four girls to help them demonstrate the steps. They arranged each child with a partner, like this:

Alison	Beth
Aaron	Benny
Claire	Dinah
Colin	Duane

For the first move, Aaron and Benny change places, and Colin and Duane change places. In the next move, Alison and Claire change places, and so do Dinah and Beth. Now, which children are partners?

NAME_______________________

Problem-Solving Strategies

We have been learning several strategies to help us solve problems.
- **Estimating** means making a reasonable guess and checking to see if our answer makes sense.
- **Act It Out** and **Make a Model** are ways of making problems more real, so that we can "see" the answer.
- **Solve a Simpler Problem** means that sometimes a difficult problem has an easier problem hidden in it. We can solve the easier problem and then **Work Backwards** to solve the original problem.

We thought you might like to try some of these strategies at home with your child.

Here are some problems similar to those we have been doing at school.

One of the best ways for your child to understand these problems is to actually solve them using real objects or making models. To help you, we have included some suggestions for ideas to use with each problem.

1. Mr. Fernandez needed some new tools for his tool box. There was a great sale at the local hardware store. Screwdrivers were $1.29, hammers $7.99, pliers $2.49, and hand saws $5.39. Mr. Fernandez bought three tools, gave the clerk $15.00, and got back $3.23 in change. What tools did he buy?

   SUGGESTION: *Use real or play money to act out this problem.*

2. To visit her sister, Miss Twitchell walks through Arcadia Forest. When she comes to the Black River, she has to cross in a very small boat. Today she has brought her cat, her mouse, and a 5-pound chunk of cheese for her sister. She can only fit herself and one other thing in the tiny boat. She can't leave her cat and mouse alone on either side of the river, because the cat would eat the mouse. She can't leave the mouse alone with the cheese, because cheese is its favorite food. How can she get all three things across the river, and how many trips will it take?

SUGGESTION: *Try acting out this problem.*

3. Here are several different views of the same cube. The cube has a number on each of its six faces. Can you tell what numbers are missing in the last two pictures?

SUGGESTION: *Make a cube from paper. Number each side as in the illustrations. To make a paper cube, cut out a shape as shown, and fold along the dotted lines.*

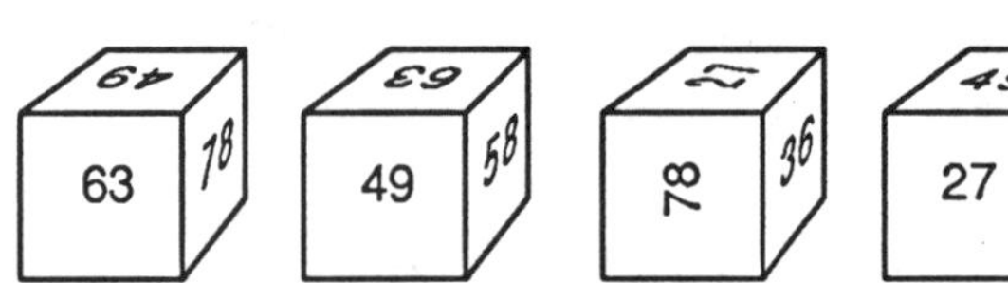 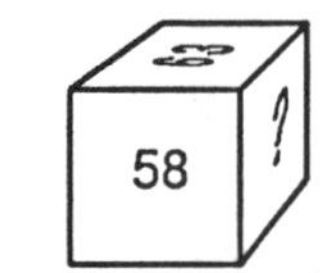 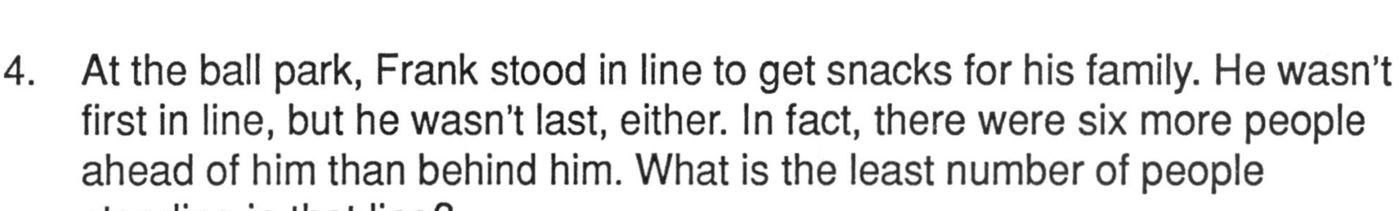

4. At the ball park, Frank stood in line to get snacks for his family. He wasn't first in line, but he wasn't last, either. In fact, there were six more people ahead of him than behind him. What is the least number of people standing in that line?

SUGGESTION: *Try acting out this problem, or making a drawing.*

                                    Unit 2 • **For You and Your Family**

UNIT 3

STRATEGY: Guess and Check

In this unit, there are problems that ask you to find combinations of numbers. One good way to start is to pick a number that seems possible. In other words, make a good guess. Then check to see if your guess was right.

How do you check? You decide if your answer matches the problem.

You may have to make several guesses before you find the right answer!

Strategy Steps:

1. Read the problem to find out as much information as possible.
2. Make a guess.
3. Check your guess with the problem.
4. Guess and check again until you find the right answer.

Stack 'Em Up

1. Mark stacked the number blocks neatly in order. Jason came along and found that he could move just one block and have all three stacks add up to the same number. How did he do it?

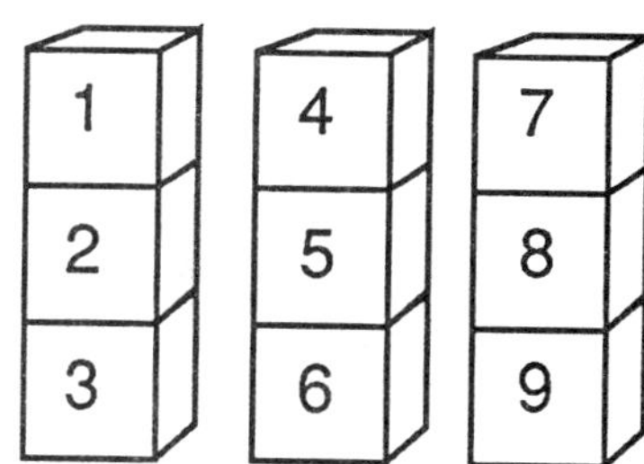

   THINK: *Which stack should he take a block from?*
   Which stack should he move it to?
   Which block should he move?

2. Anita discovered that she could take the same nine blocks and put them in five stacks so that each stack had the same sum. How did she arrange the stacks?

3. Tanya put the blocks back the way Mark had stacked them. Then she said, "I can move just one block and still have three stacks. The sum of the first stack will be two less than the second stack. The sum of the third stack will be two more than the second stack." How can she do this?

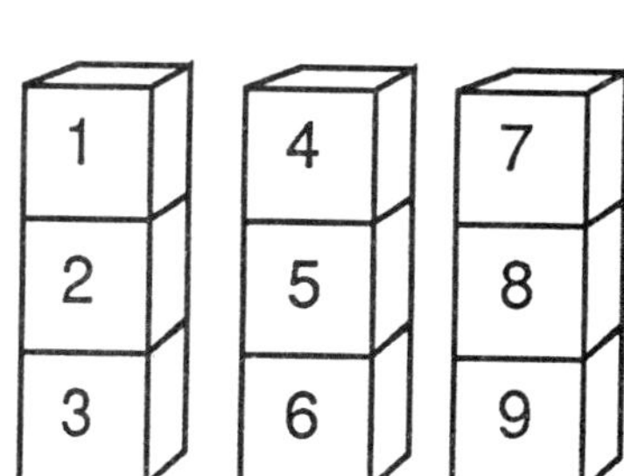

4. Derek decided he didn't like stacks, so he put the blocks in order in a line.

He told Maria that he could put in some addition signs (+) to make the sum of the blocks 99. Can he do it?

5. Gupta made a square out of the nine blocks. How did he arrange them so that the sum of the blocks was 15 in every direction – across, down, and diagonally?

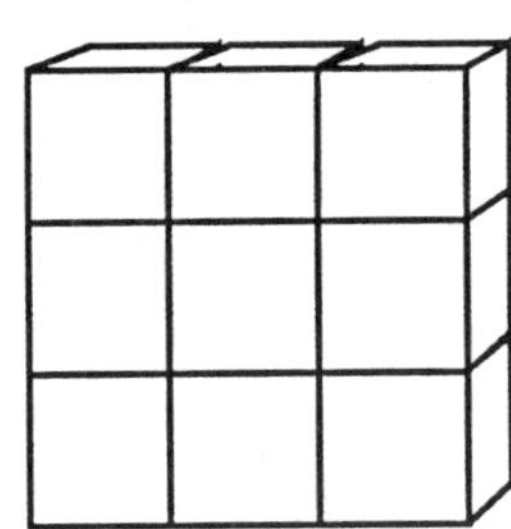

NAME_______________________

Collections

1. Victor has 24 seashells in his collection. He put them into three piles. The number of shells in each pile is in counting order. How many shells did he put in each pile?

   THINK: *How many numbers will be needed in the answer?*
   What must be the sum of those numbers?

2. Margo's three fish tanks hold a total of 30 gallons of water. The largest tank holds as much as the other two tanks together. The smallest tank holds 3 gallons less than the middle tank. How many gallons does each tank hold?

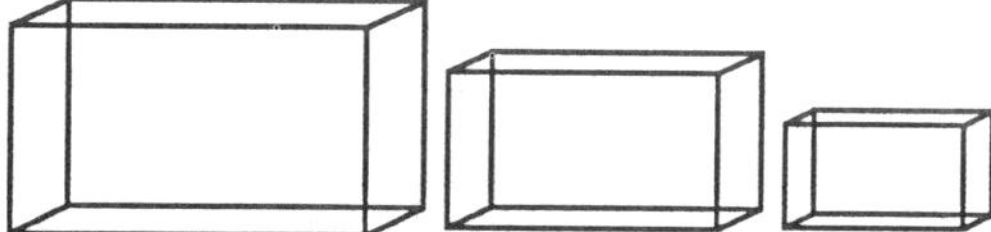

3. Margo has 66 fish in her three tanks. There are 5 more fish in the middle tank than in the largest tank and 5 more fish in the smallest tank than in the middle tank. How many fish are there in each tank?

4. Yoshi has two ant farms. One farm has red ants and the other has black ants. Yoshi has 84 ants in all. There are 16 more red ants than black ants. How many of each color does Yoshi have?

5. The third graders have been making a leaf collection. They counted a total of 126 leaves. They found that there were 23 more oak leaves than maple leaves, but 32 more maple leaves than elm leaves. How many of each kind of leaf did the children collect?

Around Town

1. Last month the Springfield city garage did 23 repair jobs. The crews repaired 7 more garbage trucks than fire trucks. How many of each did they repair?

   THINK: *What will the total number of repairs be? What strategy can you use to help you find a solution?*

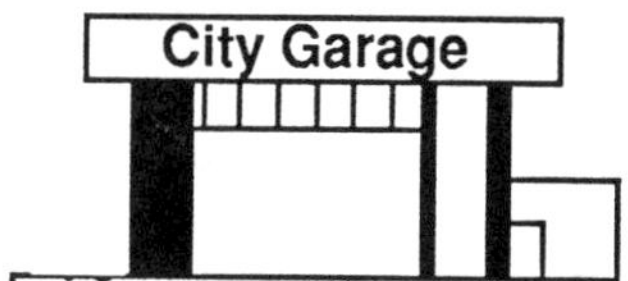

2. In Springfield there are 13 public fields for sports. There are as many soccer fields as football fields, but one more baseball field than either soccer or football fields. How many fields does Springfield have for each sport?

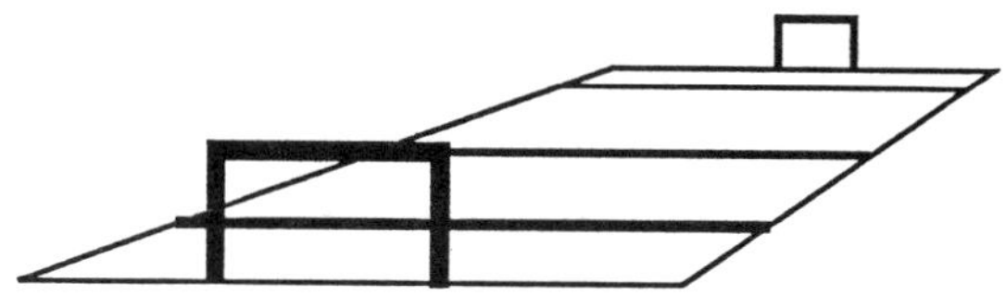

3. Together the Springfield Police and Fire Department have 75 officers. The Police Department has one more officer than the Fire Department. How many officers are there in each department?

4. During February, the librarians at the Springfield Library ordered 28 new books. The first two weeks, they ordered the same number of books. The last two weeks, they also ordered the same number of books, but it was a smaller number than the first two weeks. Each week they ordered an odd number of books, but never more than 10. How many books did they order each week?

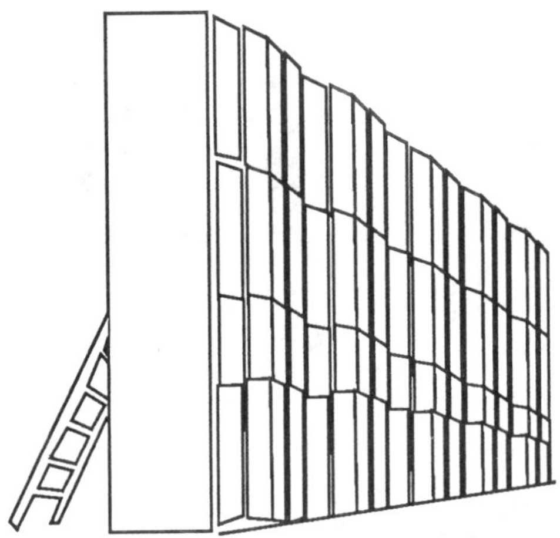

5. Each week there are 16 flights from the Springfield Airport to Washington. The flights are on Monday, Wednesday, and Friday. The most flights are on Monday. The fewest flights are on Wednesday. There is one less flight on Friday than on Monday. How many flights are there each day?

NAME_______________________

Small Change

1. Valerie and her brother Edward took the bus downtown to do some shopping. Bus fare was 65¢ for each of them. Edward had just enough change to pay both fares. He used 10 coins in all, but no half-dollars or pennies. What were the coins that he used?

   THINK: *What was the total fare?*
   What coins could he use?
   Did he use more than one of some coins?

2. At the snack shop, Valerie spent 32¢ for crackers, 49¢ for a cheese stick, and 15¢ for a fruit snack. She gave the clerk the exact amount. If she used 13 coins, what were they?

3. Edward and Valerie wanted to buy presents for their brother. Together they had $20.00. They bought two gifts at the sports shop and still had $3.00 left. What gifts did they buy?

SALE PRICES	
Soccer Ball	$8.00
Baseball Bat	$6.00
Football Helmet	$12.00
Hockey Stick	$9.00

4. Next they went to the Post Office. Edward mailed four postcards and letters for his mother. Stamps cost 29¢ for letters and 19¢ for postcards. Edward spent 96¢ for stamps. How many letters did he mail? How many postcards?

5. When they got home, Valerie had 51¢ left. She had five coins. What coins did she have?

Challenge

1. Yoki left her book open on her desk. Her mother noticed that the page numbers added up to 97. What were the two pages?

2. The license plate on Mr. Watson's car has four digits. The sum of the digits is 18. The digits are in counting order. What is his license number?

3. Charlene went to the sale at the clothing store. She had $40.00 from her birthday. She bought four things and had $2.00 left over. What did she buy?

SALE!	
Blouses	$8.00
Skirts	$10.00
Sweaters	$12.00
Jeans	$15.00

4. Vito is thinking of two numbers. The sum of the numbers is 64. The difference between them is 8. What are the numbers?

5. Put each of the numbers 1 through 6 in a circle so that each side of the triangle adds up to 9.

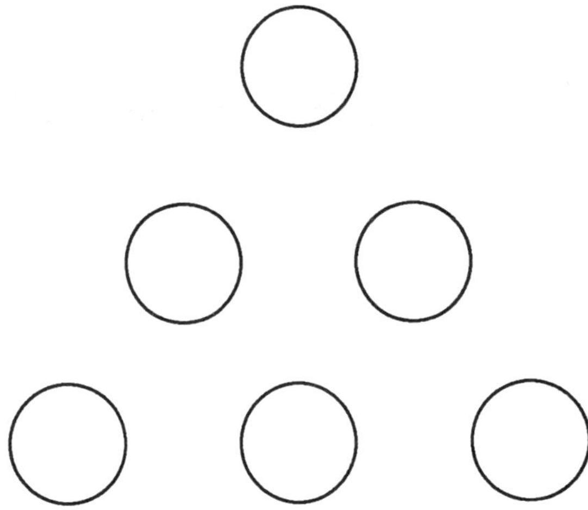

NAME_______________________

Guess and Check

In our work with problem solving, we have been learning about a strategy called *Guess and Check*. This strategy helps us solve many different problems. It works like this:

1. Read the problem carefully.
2. Make a reasonable guess at an answer.
3. Check your answer to see if it works.
4. Guess again, until you find the correct answer.

We've learned that it helps to keep track of our guesses so that each time we guess, we can come closer to the answer. A wrong guess may tell us that we need to use a larger or smaller number in our next guess.

Here are some problems for you and your child to work on together. Try using the "Guess and Check" strategy to solve them. You might want to record each guess to help you keep track of it. Making a model or drawing of the problem may also help.

1. Kesha and her father counted 66 cars in a parking lot. There were 12 more green cars than red cars, and 15 more blue cars than green cars. How many cars of each color were there?

2. Marla opened a book and noticed that the sum of the two page numbers she saw was 129. What were the two pages?

3. The sum of two numbers is 134. The difference between the two numbers is 38. What are the two numbers?

4. William has 8 coins that total to 73¢. What coins does he have?

UNIT 4

STRATEGY: Draw a Picture

Some problems are easier to solve if you can "see" what they mean. We can use the details in a problem to make pictures in our heads.

Or, we can actually make a drawing to help us solve a problem. The problems in this unit will be easier to solve if you first take time to make a picture to help you find the solution.

You don't have to be a great artist. A simple drawing will do. Just make sure your drawing matches the information in the problem.

Strategy Steps:

1. Read the whole problem.
2. Decide what kind of picture might help.
3. Make your drawing, and check to be sure it has the right information.
4. Use your picture or diagram to help you find the solution.

NAME________________________

Around Our School

1. In front of the Madison School is a row of flagpoles with flags of the different countries from which the children come. The United States flag is at one end of the school, and the flag of Western Samoa is at the other end. In between are flags of Haiti, Italy, Mexico, and Vietnam. The flagpoles are 5 meters apart. How far is it from the United States flag to the flag of Western Samoa?

    THINK: *Can you draw a picture to show all of the flagpoles in a row? How far apart are the flagpoles? How many are there?*

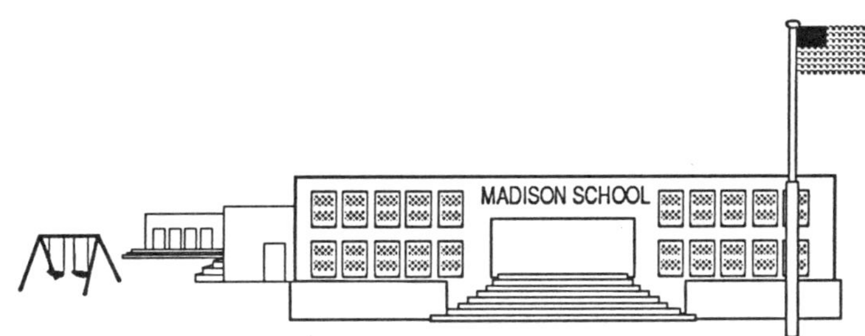

2. The King School also has several flagpoles, along one side of the playground. The playground is 200 feet long and the poles are 20 feet apart. How many flagpoles are there, if they go from end to end of the playground?

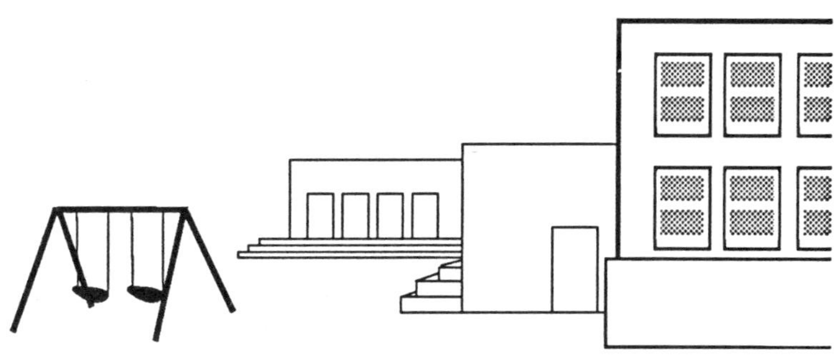

3. Along one side of the hallway are the classrooms of Ms. Walker, Mr.
    Torres, Mrs. Fujiwara, and Miss Calins. Mrs. Fujiwara's room and Ms.
    Walker's room each touch only one other classroom. What are the
    different possible orders for the classrooms?

    HINT: *Draw a picture.*
    Use W for Ms. Walker.
    Use T for Mr. Torres.
    Use F for Mrs. Fujiwara.
    Use C for Miss Calins.

4. The King School principal asked Margaret and Kareem to arrange 3
    chairs on the stage for the speakers at the Presidents' Day program. She
    told them to be sure that each chair was either directly behind, beside, or
    in front of another chair, and that all faced the audience. How many
    ways can they arrange the 3 chairs?

5. If the principal asks them to add a fourth chair, how many ways can the
    chairs be arranged?

Columbus Day

1. Christopher Columbus had three ships – the *Niña*, the *Pinta*, and the *Santa María*. The *Pinta* was not the smallest. Two of the ships were smaller than the *Santa María*. Which ship was largest? Which was smallest?

   THINK: *Can you make a drawing to show the three ships in a line, from largest to smallest?*

2. One day the three ships were sailing in a row. The largest ship was between the other two ships. The smallest ship was not the leader. In what order were the ships sailing?

3. After sailing for many weeks, Columbus and his crew saw several signs that land was near. They saw a branch with green leaves floating in the water, and a flock of birds in the sky. The first sign wasn't in the water. Finally, they saw two men in a canoe. What did they see first? What sign did they see next? What did they see last?

4. Columbus asked some of the crew to draw a map of the island where they landed. The sailors found that there was a large rock 200 paces south of a stream. They discovered a cave 500 paces north of the stream. Then, 50 paces north of the stream, they saw a tall palm tree. Was the palm tree closer to the cave or to the rock?

5. Columbus sailed to the Americas four times. On different trips he visited Puerto Rico, Central America, South America, and San Salvador. He saw San Salvador before he saw South America. He landed at three places before Central America. Puerto Rico was the second place he visited. Where did he visit on his first trip? On his second trip? On his third trip? On his fourth trip?

NAME____________________

How Does Your Garden Grow?

1. Lara planted several rows of peas in her garden. If there were eight rows to the right of the middle row, how many rows of peas did she plant?

   THINK: *What is a "middle" row? How many rows would be on each side of it?*

2. One day her brother Colin was standing at the middle row of his strawberry plants. He walked three rows to the left to pull a weed. Then he walked ten rows to the right, to the last row of strawberries. How many rows of strawberry plants were there?

3.   Lara, Colin, and their sister Kelly each grew a pumpkin vine. Lara's vine had more pumpkins than Colin's. Colin's had fewer than Kelly's. Whose vine had the fewest pumpkins?

4.   Can you tell whose vine had the most pumpkins?

5.   Kelly's part of the family garden is divided into four sections, like this:

Section 1 Beans	Section 2 Squash
Section 3 Cucumbers	Section 4 Tomatoes

Kelly's dad told her that she shouldn't plant cucumbers right next to squash. He also said that she shouldn't plant tomatoes in the same place two years in a row. How many different ways could she arrange her part of the garden next year?

It's a Date!

1. This year, the Fourth of July was a Friday. Ten days later, Bill left on a camping trip with his family. On what day and date did they leave?

   THINK: *What kind of picture would show dates and days of the week?*

2. Valentine's Day is February 14. This year Valentine's Day was a Saturday. Chung's birthday is 12 days before Valentine's Day. What day and date was his birthday?

3. Milly's birthday is August 7. Patty went to her birthday party that day. The next day, Patty went to spend two weeks with her grandmother. Peter's birthday party is on August 18. Will Patty be home in time for Peter's party?

4. Every other Monday, the third grade class takes a field trip. If they took a field trip on March 17, when will their next three trips be?

5. Carla's birthday is September 11. Her friend Sulim's birthday is October 7. Is Sulim's birthday the same day of the week as Carla's?

Challenge

1. Mrs. Warner wants to put up a fence that is 24 feet long. She plans to put a fence post every 3 feet. How many posts will she need?

2. Her neighbor, Mr. Lindstrom, has a rectangular garden that measures 20 feet by 40 feet. If he puts fence posts every 4 feet all the way around, how many posts will he need?

3. Marla was standing in the middle of the line waiting for the school bus. There were six children ahead of her. How many children were in the line?

4. Paco is taller than Liz but shorter than Cheryl. Kim is shorter than Cheryl but taller than Paco. Who is the tallest, and who is the shortest?

5. Last year, summer began on Tuesday, June 21. Fall began on September 21. What day of the week was that?

NAME_______________________

Draw a Picture

Drawing a picture is a useful way to help us solve problems. We can use a drawing to "see" the problem more clearly. The **Draw a Picture** strategy works like this:

1. Read the whole problem.
2. Decide what kind of picture would help you to understand the problem.
3. Draw a picture using the information in the problem.
4. Use the picture to help you find the solution.

Here are some problems for you and your child to try to help you explore this problem-solving strategy together.

1. Last year July 4 was a Thursday. If Claire's birthday is ten days before the holiday, what is the date of her birthday and what day of the week was it last year?

2. There are six posts from one end to the other of the fence behind Mr. Rayford's vegetable garden. If the posts are six feet apart, how long is the fence?

3. Roberto's brother parked his car in the middle space in a row of parking spaces at the mall. If there were seven spaces to the left of the space where he parked, how many spaces were there in that row?

4. The highway from Dry Gulch to Cactus City runs for 200 km straight across the desert. Along the way are three towns: Lonesome Pine, Gopher Town, and Coyote Junction. Here are some road signs you can see while driving from Dry Gulch to Cactus City:

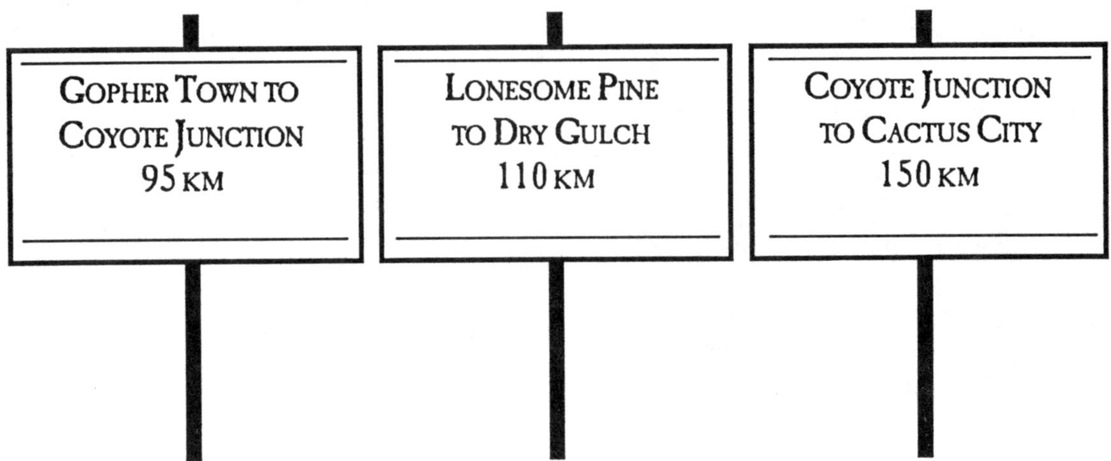

In what order would you pass through the three towns on your way from Dry Gulch to Cactus City?

5. How far is it from
    a. Coyote Junction to Lonesome Pine?
    b. Dry Gulch to Gopher Town?
    c. Lonesome Pine to Cactus City?

UNIT 5

STRATEGY: Make a List

The problems in this unit will have many possible answers. Sometimes you will need to know all the possible answers. For other problems, you will have to decide which is the best answer out of all the possibilities.

One way to make sure that you have thought of all the possible answers is to make an organized list. To make an organized list, you will want to use some kind of system. Instead of just listing possibilities, your system should help you make sure that you have thought of all the possibilities.

Strategy Steps:

1. Read the whole problem.
2. Figure out a system for making sure you list all the possible answers.
3. Make your list.
4. Use your list to check your solution.

NAME_______________________

Number, Please

1. Barbara is making number tags for the coat check at the school play. If the number tags are numbered from 1 through 100, how many times will she write the numeral 3?

   THINK: *Is there a simple way to keep track of all the numbers between 1 and 100 that have a 3 in them?*

2. May can't remember the address of her new friend Akio. She knows that he lives on Archer Avenue. She remembers that his house number has only three digits in it – 3, 5, and 7 – but she doesn't know the order. How many different addresses could her friend live at?

3. The Brewster School has two floors of classrooms. The classrooms are numbered according to this system:
   • All the room numbers are three digits.
   • The digit in the hundreds place tells which floor the room is on.
   • The digit in the tens place is always less than 3.
   • The digit in the ones place is always odd.

   If all the possible combinations are used, how many classrooms are there in the school?

4. Paula and Bill bought some sew-on numerals to put on the back of the
    basketball team's shirts. The only numerals the store had in stock were
    2's, 4's, 5's, and 6's. If they sew two numerals on each shirt, can they
    make enough different numbers so that each of the 18 team members
    has a different number?

5. Cans of juice in the vending machine cost $.75. Carlos has five coins –
    just enough to buy one can of juice. What coins does he have?

NAME________________________

Adding It Up

1. At swim meets, swimmers score 5 points for winning an event, 3 points for second place, and 1 point for third place. Last week, Mitch scored points in 5 different events, and earned a total of 17 points. How many firsts, seconds, and thirds did he score?

   THINK: *What different combinations of 5, 3, and 1 add up to exactly 17?*

2. Yesterday the Mustangs and Colts played a soccer game. During the game, a total of only 7 goals were scored. What are the possible final scores for each team?

3. Karen shot 5 arrows and hit the target each time. She scored 45 points in all. If her shots scored 3 different numbers, what were her 5 scores?

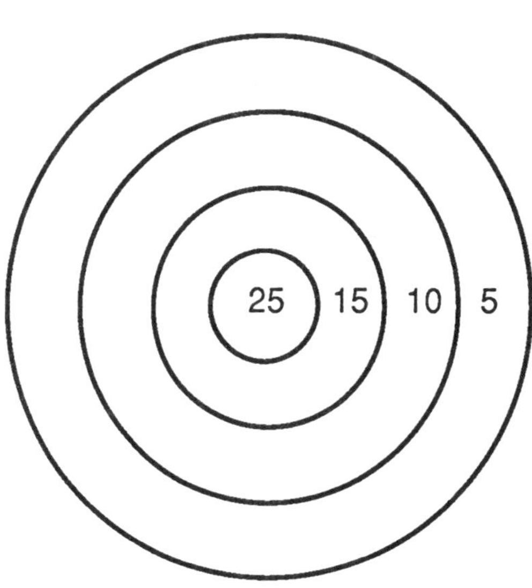

4. Last night Mike's basketball team scored between 40 and 60 points. The 2 digits in the team's score are 2 numbers apart from each other. The sum of the digits is more than 10. How many points did Mike's team score?

5. The Hurricanes scored 13 points in Tuesday's volleyball game. Jen, Lupe, and Corinne were the only players who scored. They each scored a different number of points. None of them scored as many as ten points. Lupe scored two points more than Corinne. Jen scored one point more than Lupe and Corinne scored together. How many points did each girl score?

NAME_______________________

May I Take Your Order?

1. At Vinny's Pizza Shop, a small pizza with cheese costs $2.75. For $.25 extra, you can add green peppers, onions, or mushrooms. Sausage, pepperoni, or ham costs $.50 extra. Chad has $3.50 to spend. What different combinations might he order if he spent all his money?

    THINK: *How can you organize a list to show all the combinations he could buy? How much would each combination cost?*

2. The Ice Cream Palace has triple-dip cones on sale. Today's flavors are vanilla, chocolate, strawberry, banana, and peach. How many different combinations can Rosa order, if she asks for 3 different flavors?

3. Here is today's menu in the cafeteria:

    Today's Choices

Sandwich	Side Dish	Drink
Hamburger	Salad	Milk
Grilled Cheese	Fruit cup	Fruit Punch

    There are 19 children in Ms. Wilson's class. Can each child order a different combination for lunch if everyone chooses one item from each column?

4. At Harry's Hot Dog Stand, you can get ketchup, mustard, relish, and onions on your hot dog. How many different ways could Harry serve his hot dogs?

5. The Great Southwest Barbecue Pit offers 4 choices of meat: beef, chicken, ribs, and sausage. They also have 4 side dishes: corn, cole slaw, potato salad, and baked beans. Today's special is the famous Combination Plate, which has 3 different meats and 2 different side dishes. How many different Combination Plates could the restaurant make up?

Choices and Combinations

1. Trans-America Airlines is offering special vacation fares to families in Atlanta, where Benny lives. On this special fare, you can visit New York and any two other cities on this list:

   Boston   Chicago   Denver   Phoenix   Los Angeles

   How many different trips could Benny and his family plan on this special fare?

   THINK: *How many combinations of two other cities can you put with New York?*

2. According to the map below, how many different routes can Ramon and his family take from their home in Lakeside to his grandmother's house in Ocean City?

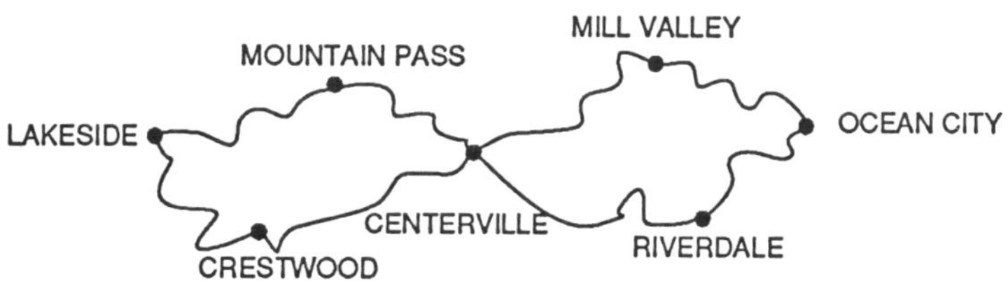

3. During the morning rush hours, from 6:30 a.m. to 9:30 a.m., westbound trains arrive at the Beverly station every 15 minutes. Eastbound trains arrive there every 30 minutes during that time. At 6:30 a.m., both an eastbound train and a westbound train arrive at the Beverly station. During the morning rush hours, how many different westbound and eastbound trains will arrive?

4. How many times will an eastbound and a westbound train arrive at the same time at the Beverly station during the morning rush hours?

5. Melissa planned a trip from her home in Westerly to visit her cousins in Columbus. Using the map below, she decided to use as many means of transportation as possible. What route did she take, and how many different means of transportation did she use?

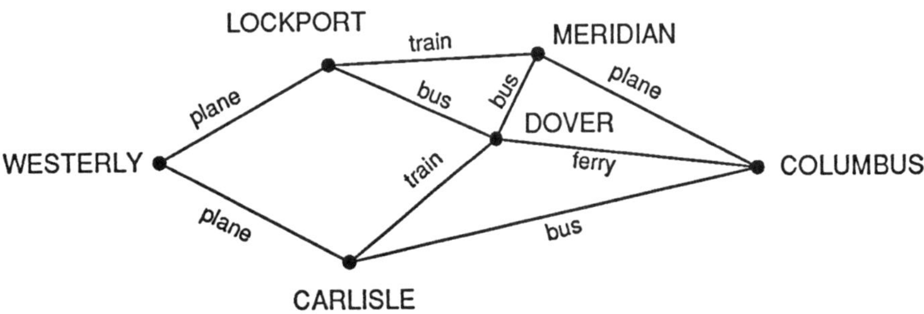

Challenge

1. Ellen and Shamir are planning for the school fair. They want to set up 3 food booths – one for hot dogs, one for popcorn, and one for drinks. How many ways can they arrange the 3 booths in a row?

2. At the library book sale, hardcover books are $.50 and paperbacks are 3 for $.25. Marla spent $2.00 to buy 9 books. How many of each kind did she buy?

3. If a computer prints out all the numbers from 0 to 1000, how many times will it print out the digit "1"?

4. There are seven rides at the Shoreline Amusement Park. They are the
    Ferris Wheel, the Roller Coaster, the Bumper Cars, the Pony Rides, the
    Magic Twirler, the Water Slide, and the Flying Saucer. Billy buys a special
    ticket good for any three rides. How many different combinations of rides
    can he choose from, if he does not repeat a ride?

5. King Midas wants to divide his 15 chests of gold among his 4 children so
    that the oldest gets more than the next oldest and so on. Knowing that the
    king doesn't want to split up any of the chests and that he doesn't want
    any of his children to have more than 10 chests, his wise old minister tells
    him that there are six different ways he can divide his gold. Is the minister
    right?

NAME________________________

Make a List

Sometimes problems have many possible answers. In some cases, we need to know how many possible answers there are. At other times, we may need to know which answer out of the possible answers is best.

We have been using a strategy called **Make a List** to help us solve these kinds of problems. Usually this strategy takes 3 steps:

1. Find a system for listing all the possibilities.
2. Make a complete list.
3. Use the list to check for the best solution – that is, the one that fits the problem exactly.

Here are some problems like the ones we have been doing in class for you and your child to do together.

1. Mr. Parker wanted new house numbers to put on his house. He went to the store and bought three large wooden numbers: a 7, a 3, and a 4. Mr. Parker lives on Woodland Avenue, but what could his house number be? How many different possibilities are there?

    SUGGESTION: *Try writing each number on a piece of paper and arranging them in different orders.*

2. At the school fair, Kim and Lila entered the baseball toss contest. Lila hit
    the target each of her four tosses and scored a total of 50 points. Did she
    ever hit the center section of the target?

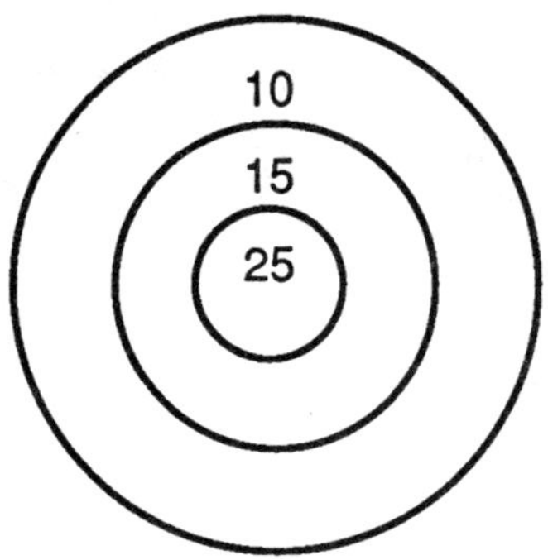

3. Kim also scored a total of 50 points, hitting the target three out of four
    tries. What were her three scores?

4. Jamul needs 80¢ for the bus. In his drawer he found six coins, just
    enough for the bus. What were the coins?

    SUGGESTION: *Try using coins to help you.*

UNIT 6

STRATEGY: Look for a Pattern

Suppose you could only see half of a checkerboard. Could you tell what the other half looked like? Probably you could, because you know that the pattern of red and black squares will continue on the half you can't see.

Many problems can be solved by finding a pattern and using that pattern to find a solution.

In this unit you will look for patterns, figure out what the pattern is, and decide what comes next.

Strategy Steps:

1. Look for a pattern.
2. Decide what changes in the pattern.
3. Figure out what comes next.
4. Check to see if the pattern is still the same.

NAME _______________________

Patterns Everywhere

1. Continue the pattern.

> **THINK:** *What pattern do you see?*
> *What part of the pattern repeats?*
> *What figures would you use to continue the pattern?*

a. 

b. 

c. 

d. ⊕ ⊕ ⊕ ⊕ ⊕ ___ ___ ___

2. Use patterns to help you fill in the missing words.

a. walk, walked; look, looked; paint, _______________; talk, _______________

b. book, books; truck, trucks; toy, _______________; lamp, _______________

c. tall, taller, tallest; long, longer, longest; small, _______________, _______________

d. neat, messy; early, late; shut, _______________; day, _______________

3. Continue the pattern. Talk about how you found the pattern.

   a. 14, 16, 18, 20, ____, ____, ____

   b. 42, 39, 36, 33, ____, ____, ____

   c. 68, 75, 82, 89, ____, ____, ____

   d. 1, 2, 4, 8, ____, ____, ____, ____

4. Continue the pattern. Talk about the pattern.

   a. 206, 207, 209, 212, 216, ____, ____, ____

   b. 13, 16, 21, 28, 37, ____, ____, ____

   c. 332, 324, 317, 311, 306, ____, ____, ____

   d. 98, 96, 92, 86, 78, ____, ____, ____

5. Continue the pattern. Talk about the pattern.

   a. 17, 20, 19, 22, 21, ____, ____, ____, ____

   b. 36, 43, 40, 47, 44, ____, ____, ____, ____

Flying South

Every year, flocks of birds fly south over Midland City on their way to spend the winter in a warmer climate.

Carmen and Luis noticed that each flock passing overhead was led by one bird. In the next row were two birds, then three, then four, and so on. Luis made this picture to show how all the flocks looked:

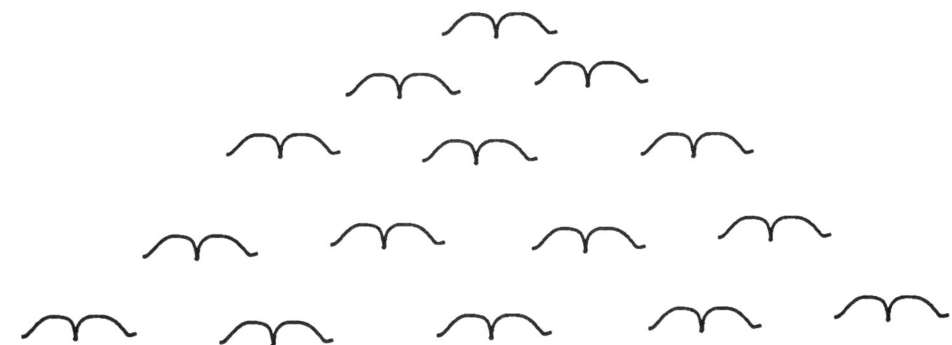

1. How many birds did Carmen count in the next row, which Luis did not put in his picture? If Luis counted the row after that, how many birds would he see in it?

   THINK: How many birds in the first row? In the second row? Would it help to draw a picture of the next row? How many birds would be in the row?

2. Luis saw a flock of birds that was in seven rows. How many birds were there in the flock?

3. Perry counted 45 birds in one flock. How many rows were there?

4. Some of the birds stop at Long Lake near Midland City. On Saturday, 2 birds landed at the lake. On Sunday, 4 birds joined them. On Monday, 8 more birds arrived. Tuesday, the flock increased by 16. If this pattern continued, how many birds were in the flock by Friday night?

5. On Sunday, there were 84 birds at the lake, but 3 flew away. On Monday, 6 flew off. On Tuesday, 9 more flew off. If that pattern continued, on what day would the last birds fly away?

Getting in Shape

The members of the Marathon Club are planning how they will train for the long-distance race. Everyone will start training on the same day. They will all run 5 kilometers the first day of training, but then each person's plan is different. However, no one will ever run more than 26 kilometers in a day.

Here is a chart showing how many kilometers some of the members will run for the first few days:

Runner	Day 1	Day 2	Day 3	Day 4	Day 5
Tanya	5	8	11	14	17
Joan	5	6	8	11	15
Peter	5	6	8	9	11

1. How many kilometers will each of these members run on Day 6?

   THINK: *What are the differences between the terms in each runner's plan? Are they all the same?*

2. Tell how each runner plans to increase his or her distance each day. Look for a pattern in the chart.

   Tanya ____

   Joan ____

   Peter ____

3. If Peter starts this training on Monday, how many kilometers will he be running by the following Monday?

    HINT: *Use the chart. Continue the number pattern.*

4. If the runners follow their plan to increase their distance each day, which runner will be the first to reach 26 kilometers a day? Which runner will be the last to reach 26 kilometers a day?

5. On the day when Tanya first runs 26 kilometers, how many kilometers will Peter run?

Computer Games

The third graders have been learning to use the new program in the Computer Center. The computer can print out number patterns like this, depending on the command:

15, 17, 19, 21, 23

For example, if the command is to start with 1 and add 2 each time, the computer will print this:

1, 3, 5, 7, 9, 11, and so on.

1. Suppose the command is to start with 87 and subtract 3 each time. What are the first five numbers the computer will print out?

   THINK: *What number should we start with?*
   How many times should we subtract?

2. One day, Max printed out this number pattern:

   0, 2, 6, 12, 20

   What will the next three numbers in the pattern be?
   What command did Max give?

3. Leona printed out a different number pattern:

$$1, 4, 9, 16, 25$$

What commands did she give?

What will be the next three numbers in her pattern?

4. Rory found that he could program the computer to perform the same operation on a series of numbers. When Rory input 37, the computer printed out 44. Here are some other numbers Rory worked with. What command did he use?

Input	22	56	81
Printout	29	63	88

Here are some more numbers Rory put into the computer.
What will the computer print out for these inputs?

Input	178	212	324
Printout			

5. Mei-ling used a two-step command. Here is part of the printout:

Input	14	39	52	80	112	1,056
Printout	22	72	98			

What comand did she use?

What will the next three numbers in her pattern be?

Challenge

1. Meredith has been saving pennies. She stacked them up with one penny in the first stack, two pennies in the second stack, three pennies in the third stack, and so on. If she has $1.53 in pennies, how many stacks did she make?

2. Find the number pattern. Complete the chart.

1	2	4	8	
2	4	8		
4	8			
8				

3. Joe and Alva work each day at the Pizza Palace. They can each make 12 pizzas every 10 minutes. One afternoon, the principal of Fleetwood School called in an order for 120 pizzas for the school party. How long did it take for Joe and Alva to fill the order?

4. In Larry's apartment building, there are six apartments on each side of the
    hallway. Each apartment door is directly opposite another apartment door.
    On the north side of the hallway, the first apartment door is white, the
    second door is blue, the third door is white, and so on. On the south side
    of the hall, the first apartment door is red, the second door is gray, the
    third door is red, and so on. Larry lives in the fifth apartment on the south
    side. What color is the apartment door opposite his? What color are the
    doors of the apartments on each side of his?

5. Alana programmed her computer to start with 87, subtract 3 four times,
    and then add 7 four times. What will be the ninth number her computer
    prints out?

Look for a Pattern

We've discovered that solving some problems is much easier if you use a strategy called *look for a pattern.*

When we use this strategy, we try to find a pattern to help us solve the problem. We check to see what changes from one part of the pattern to the next. Then we try to find what comes next in the pattern. To check our answer, we see if it fits the pattern.

Here are some problems for you to try with your child.

1. Continue the pattern.

    a. 

    b. 

    c. 

2. Mrs. Watson asked Marla to baby sit for her two children from 3:30 to 6:00 Monday through Friday afternoon for the next two weeks. Mrs. Watson offered to pay Marla either $5.00 a day or $1.00 the first day, $2.00 the second day, $3.00 the third day, and so on. Which way would Marla earn more money?

3. Continue the pattern.

a. 2, 9, 16, 23, ____ , ____ , ____ , ____

b. 381, 382, 384, 387, ____ , ____ , ____ , ____

c. 210, 201, 193, 186, ____ , ____ , ____ , ____

d. 43, 49, 44, 50, 45, ____ , ____ , ____ , ____

NAME________________________________

(Use after Unit 2.)
Use a strategy you have learned to help you solve the following problems.

1. Six friends want to buy drinks from the vending machine. They have a
   total of 16 quarters to spend. If they spend all their money, can everyone
   get a drink? How many will drink milk, and how many will drink juice?

   HINT: Use real or play coins to help.

MILK	50¢
JUICE	75¢
(Apple, Orange, Grape)	

2. Put the numbers 1, 2, 3, 4, 5, and 6 in the circles so that the three
   numbers on each side of the triangle have a sum of 9. You must use all
   the numbers, so no number is used more than once.

   *HINT: Write each number on a paper circle. Move the circles around until
   you find the correct sums.*

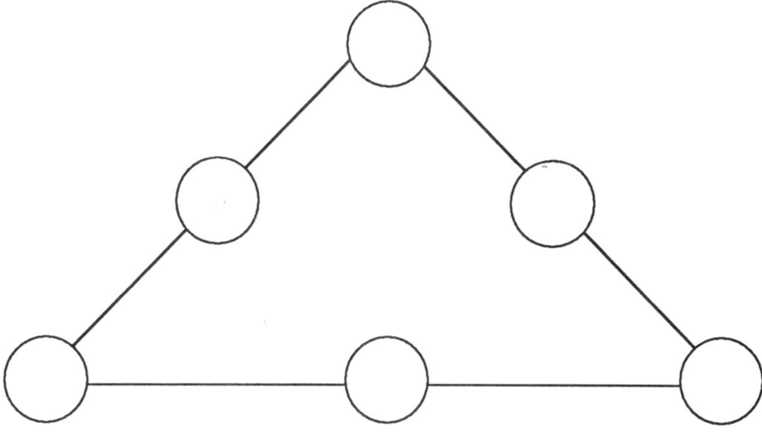

3. Six members of the Saturday Movie Club got to the theatre very early to make sure they were at the front of the line. They lined up like this:

Alyssa   Bennett   Chip   Doreen   Ed   Felipe

The children had to wait a long time before the ticket booth opened, so they started playing a game. First, Alyssa and Felipe changed places in line. Then, Ed and Bennett changed places. Next, Chip and Doreen changed places. Finally, Felipe and Chip changed places while Alyssa and Doreen also changed places.

Now, how were the children lined up?

HINT: *Cut out paper models to help you.*

NAME_______________________

(Use after Unit 3.)

1. Luann was making a design for the school mural. Her design looked like this:

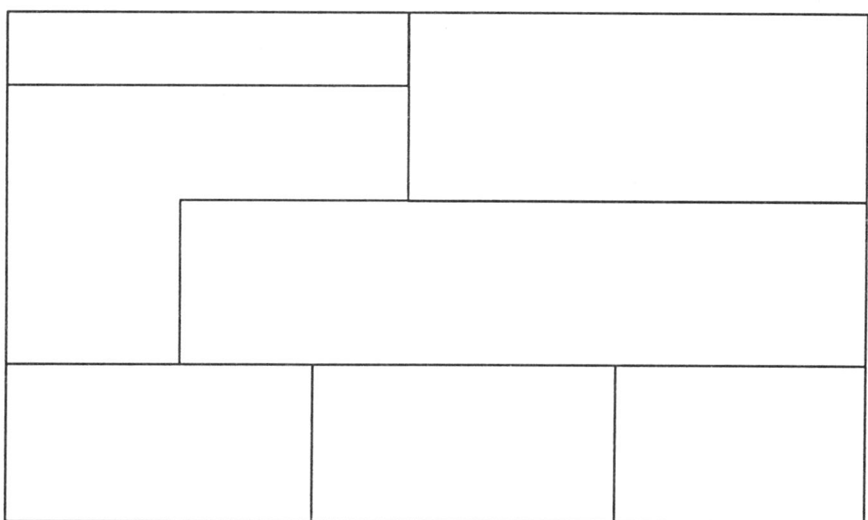

   She decided to paint the design so that any two areas that touched would be different colors. Luann has blue paint and yellow paint, the school colors. Does she have enough colors to paint her design the way she wants to?

   HINT: *To see if the plan works, write b (blue) and y (yellow) in the design.*

   Ming Chin liked Luann's design, and offered to help her with it. If she has some red paint, can the girls finish the design using Luann's plan? If the plan works, color the design.

2. Barry, Kumi, and Ariel put all their money together to buy a card for their friend. Barry had 50¢, Kumi had 55¢, and Ariel had 45¢. Together they had 12 coins – just enough for the card. What coins did each child have?

   HINT: Use real or play coins to help.

3. Read the clues. Find the numbers.
   a. The sum of two numbers is 157. The difference between the two numbers is 11. What are the numbers?

   b. The sum of two numbers is 57. The difference between the two numbers is 15. What are the numbers?

   c. The sum of two numbers is 101. The difference between the two numbers is 17. What are the numbers?

      HINT: Use paper and pencil to keep track of the numbers you try. Use a calculator to add and subtract.

(Use after Unit 4.)

1. Three of Michelle's friends planned a surprise party for her. Kayla spent $2.00 for invitations. Velma bought the decorations for $8.00, and Luisa spent $5.00 for refreshments. How can the three girls make sure that each one pays the same amount for the party?

   HINT: Use play money to help you.

2. Marie received an invitation to the party, and went to the shopping center to buy Michelle a present. She found several things she liked: a book for $6.00, hair ribbons for $2.00, a soccer ball for $5.00, and a picture frame for $3.00. She chose two of the gifts, and gave the clerk $10.00. She got back $3.00 in change. What did Marie buy?

   HINT: Use play money to help you.

3. Coach Babson asked the basketball team to line up by height, tallest first. On the team, Jack is shorter than Paco. Ryan is taller than three of the boys. Eddie is taller than Paco, and four of the boys are taller than Alberto. How should the team line up?

   HINT: *Make a drawing to help you.*

4. Manuel's father plans to tile their basement floor. The basement is a rectangle 12 feet by 15 feet. The tiles are 1-foot squares. Manuel wanted to put a green-tile border around the room. The border would be one tile wide. The rest of the tiles would be white. How many green tiles would they need?

   HINT: *Use Unifix cubes if available, or make a model of your own to help you.*

Expert Problems

NAME_______________________________

(Use after Unit 5.)

1. The science teacher asked Sandra to go to the storeroom and bring out some weights for the science experiment. She found a stack of six weights. Each weight was 2 kilograms heavier than the one on top of it. If the bottom weight was 20 kilograms, how much did the whole stack weigh?

   HINT: Make a model of the weights to help you.

2. The photographer arranged the team members so he could get all of them into the picture. He put one person in the first row, two in the second, three in the third, and so on. If there were eight rows in all, how many team members were there?

   HINT: Act it out, or make a model to help you.

3. The Crosstown bus stops at Hayne's Drug Store every 45 minutes. It is now 2:30. A bus stopped half an hour ago. How many more times will the bus stop before the store closes at 7:00?

    HINT: *Use a clock to help you.*

4. Mark is making a poster for the Spring Fair. He is using a sheet of cardboard 24 inches high and 36 inches wide. He decides to use letters that are 2 inches high, and leave a 1-inch space between each of the lines. He also decides to have a 2-inch border all the way around the poster. How many lines of letters can he fit on his poster?

    HINT: *Draw a picture to help you.*

NAME____

(Use after Unit 6.)

1. Fred began a weight-lifting program. Each day he lifted 5 pounds more than the day before. On the fifth day of training, he lifted 70 pounds. How many did he lift on the tenth day? How many pounds did he lift in all during the ten days?

   HINT: *Make a table to help you.*

2. Rosie and Gloria each had a number riddle.

   Gloria's riddle:
   My number has three digits. The digits have a sum of 18. If you subtract the middle digit from the first digit, the difference is the third digit.
   What is Gloria's number?

   Rosie's riddle:
   I'm thinking of two numbers. If you add them, the sum is 169. The difference between them is 27.
   What are Rosie's numbers?

   HINT: *Use pencil and paper to keep track of the numbers you try. Use a calculator to add and subtract.*

3.   Mr. and Mrs. Alonzo were visiting Bay City for the first time. One morning they went out for a walk. From their hotel they went east for several blocks. Then they turned right and went three blocks. They then turned left, but after two blocks, they realized they were going the wrong way. They turned around and went back seven blocks. They then turned right. What direction were they heading now?

HINT: *Make a drawing to help you.*

4.   Mrs. Pritchard, the school secretary, has eleven reports to type up for the principal. The principal needs the reports for a meeting at 2:00 p.m. It's now 11:00 a.m. Can Mrs. Pritchard finish the reports in time if each one takes 20 minutes, or should she ask someone to help her?

HINT: *Use a clock to help you.*

5.   The Public Library is having a sale of used books. Two books cost $1.25. Three books cost $1.65. Four books cost $2.00. Five books cost $2.30. Luis found eight books he likes. How much would he pay for the books?

HINT: *Make a table to help. Find how much the price increases with each purchase. Look for a pattern.*

Expert Problems